Shades of Life

A Collection of Poems

by

Donald W. Grant

Copyright © 2015 by Donald W. Grant

Cover design © 2015 by Lydia Mullins
Cover Photo © 2015 by D.W. Grant

Published By D2C Perspectives
All rights reserved.

No part of this book may be reproduced in any form or by any electronic or mechanical means including information storage and retrieval systems, without permission in writing from the author. The only exception is by a reviewer, who may quote short excerpts in a review.
Printed in the United States of America

ISBN 978-1-943142-06-4

Table of Contents

Introduction
Seeds of A Man 1

DARK
Father and Son 23
A Soul Bound 24
To The Past 26
From Light Into Dark 27
False image 28
Guilt 29
Abused 30
Dilemma 31
For Christ's Sake 33
From Shepherd To Snake 34
As The Light Dims 37

GRAY

The Roller Coaster 41

Reality   43
Duality   44
Stepfather   46
Perplexed   47
The Play of Life - Act One   48
Choice   50
Why?   51
To My Sister-In-Law   54
Alone   55
Memo   56
The Right   58
The Optimist In A Democracy   60
A New Beginning   61

LIGHT!

Into The Light   65
In Search of Love   67
Love Finally Found   68
At Half Moon Bay   70
Red   72
The Bay   73
Renewal   76
Face To Face   77

The Shelf   79
Technology   80
My Heart   81
Cathryn   82
Love And Struggle   83
Step One of A Marriage   85

About The Author   87

Introduction

Men are often considered unemotional. At least less emotional than women. I do not think that is true. I believe men just express their emotions differently. For me it is usually by writing my thoughts about whatever bothers, excites, or saddens me. More often than not this takes the form of poetry.

Over the years, having had a myriad of experiences and careers, I have accumulated poems that at the time expressed my feelings or opinions about life. This is a collection of those writings.

My first entry is not a poem, but a short diatribe about events in my youth that helped shape me into who I am today. *The Seeds of A Man* will, I hope, make you smile, even though it is a bit sad.

The poems are broken into sections of Dark, Gray, and Light, reflecting the emotional state I was in at the time of putting words to paper.

Interpretation is a subjective thing and I hope that as you read my collection there will be some that make you tear up, laugh, or better yet, think. Enjoy them for what they are, *Shades of Life*.

Seeds of A Man

THE STATION WAGON bounced along the dirt road, spewing a trail of red dust behind it. The road was exactly one mile long from the paved highway to my grandparents' farmhouse. In 1956 there were no seat belts and it was okay to be in the back of the car where there were no seats. Over every bump and rut, I was tossed around like a helium ballon, bumping my head on the roof, rolling around as we veered left then right. I was having a blast.

We were a family of five. My dad was career Air Force, having joined the Army-Air Corps in 1939, so we moved every couple of years, a background that makes me fearless about change. My mother was seven years younger than my dad who had just turned forty. My two sisters were fifteen and three which put me as the middle child at nine and the only boy.

So here we were, in the heat of a hot August day, in our new Chevrolet wagon making our biennial trip to North Carolina to see my grandparents on the farm where they grew cotton and peanuts. My dad had been assigned to an Air Force base in Morocco and for some reason, we couldn't go until November so we would be staying with them. The thought of running loose on forty acres and knowing my cousin Joe, who was my age, lived on the farm, had me excited.

We pulled up to the farmhouse and bailed out of the car, only to find no one around. My dad walked out to the edge of the cotton field and called back to us, "They're out picking cotton." I ran out to the field and yelled "Hey Gramma, Grandpa, Joe." They looked up, said "Hey," and went back to picking. We all walked out to where they were bent over plucking cotton bolls and my grandpa said, "Ya'll just in time, grab a sack and help out."

Now I doubt if you have ever picked cotton, but there are three terrible things about it. The sack is about twelve feet long, and to a boy four-feet-four-inches, it looked humongous. As you pick you are bent over just slightly, which for me wasn't as bad, but still not all that comfortable. But the worst is, as you pluck the cotton, you can prick your fingers on the plant if you're not careful. Oh, and as my grandmother pointed out to me several times, you better pick all the cotton and not leave tufts.

My dad told me to grab a sack, my mom said she would take my sisters to the house and unpack the car, and I started "pickin" cotton. After about an hour I said I needed to use the restroom and headed for the house. Before I could head back they all came in and said it was lunch time.

We sat down to fresh creamed corn, sticky rice, fried chicken, green beans, biscuits, and fresh milk. At home this would have been a dinner but out here it was just a hardy lunch. I ate until I couldn't swallow anymore and then my grandpa said, "Well, we better get back at it."

As we all walked back toward the field I asked my cousin if this was what he did everyday. He said, "Pretty much, until all the cotton is in." I was a skinny city boy weighing about sixty pounds, he was my height but had about fifteen pounds on me. One real difference between the two of us, since he had grown up on a farm, was even though we were the same age he was a lot stronger. A difference that later would have him go undefeated as a high school wrestler. I said, "Maybe we can sneak away when they're not looking and go down to the creek." He said, "Gramma would whip me if we tried." So off we went back to "pickin".

After about an hour and a half I told Joe I was hot and we needed to sneak off, he said no way and kept on plucking cotton bolls. I said, "Let's hide in our cotton sacks and see if they miss us." He laughed and said, "Okay.. We crawled into our twelve foot sacks and lay there snickering. It didn't take long for my grandmother to notice we were out of sight. She started calling out, " Joe, Bill, where are you two?" We laid real still and then she called out again, "Joe, if you don't come out here I'm going to whip ya." My cousin scrambled out of his sack and shouted, "Here I am." When my grandmother asked him what he was doing he said, "It was Bill's idea to hide in the sacks." I came crawling out and my dad popped me in the back of the head. -[Let me explain something here. My name is Donald William. I am named after two of my dad's best friends. I guess he liked William better because I grew up being called Bill. It wasn't until I went into the service people started calling me Don, which is how anyone after high school knew me.] By the end of the first day on the farm I had established myself as a lazy shit, not the first nor last time I made my father wonder if I was worth the time of day.

THE NEXT MORNING I woke to the sound of a rooster crowing and my grandmother yelling, "Joe, y'all get outta bed and feed the chickens." We jumped out of bed, dressed, and headed out to the chicken coup. My cousin showed me how to toss corn to the chickens and said he was going to go to the barn to milk the cow. That sounded like more fun to me but I figured I would get my chance.

As he headed off, I saw a rooster walking around the outside of the coup. He kept strutting up to the wire trying to get in. I snuck up behind him, plucked him up, opened the gate, and tossed him into the coup. He puffed out his chest like he was king of the roost but about the same time another rooster appeared crowing and puffing out his chest. Next thing I knew, I was watching a cock fight. The hens were scattering, feathers were flying everywhere, and all the noise brought my grandmother out of the house. She ran past me and went into the coup. She tore off her apron and tossed it over one of the roosters, scooped him up and came back out. She tossed him on the ground and yelled, "Shoo, get away from here."

She turned to me and said, "How did he get in there?" I said, "I put him in, I thought he had gotten out."

"He belongs to Mr. Crawford over yonder," she said. "He's always trying to get in our coup. Don't you know there is only one rooster in a chicken coup?"

"No ma'am."

"Get back in the house, it's time for breakfast." She turned toward the barn, "Joe, bring that milk in and let's eat."

As I started back to the house I looked up and saw my dad standing on the porch, shaking his head. He turned and went inside, I knew what he was thinking.—*You dumb ass.*

After breakfast my grandmother turned to my dad and said, "Clyde, how about killing a couple of chickens this morning so I can get them ready for supper. You might want to show Bill how it's done."

I figured this was my punishment.

My dad told me to come on and we headed back out to the chicken coup. He said, "Stand right here and don't move." He headed over to the barn and came back with a couple of pieces of cord and a knife as big as a machete. He put them on the ground and went into the coup. He grabbed a hen and came back out. He said, "This is how you kill a chicken, so just watch."

He proceeded to tie up the chicken's feet and string the cord over a clothesline in the yard. The chicken was flapping trying to get loos. My dad took the knife, grabbed the head, and cut it off. The headless body kept flapping as blood dripped to the ground. My dad still had the head in his hand and it too was moving. He pointed it at me and I screamed, he started chasing me around the yard, laughing and saying, "Gonna get ya." I ran into the house. My mother came out and yelled at my dad, "What are you doing to him?"

"Just playing with him", my dad said. "Tell him to come on, we need to go back out to the cotton field."

ONE POSITIVE THING about my dad was he was a practical joker, but his jokes had a mean streak to them. One year for Christmas, my mom had been asking for a dishwasher. On Christmas Eve my dad told her to go out to the garage to get some toilet paper, and as she stepped out she shrieked, "Oh my god! A dishwasher." There was a big dishwasher box sitting in the middle of the garage. We all ran out to see and as she got close, the top shot up and one of my dad's friends jumped up saying, "I'm your new dishwasher." She did get a new one, but only after tears and having the crap scared out of her.

One of his meanest jokes, was the time she asked him to watch a pot roast. She had been cooking and realized she had forgotten something she needed to finish dinner. The pot roast was in the oven and she said to my dad, "Clyde, can you keep an eye on the roast, I have to run to the store?" He said, "Sure," and off she went. My dad went into the kitchen took the roast out of the oven, scraped off some of the browner pieces on the end, and put the rest of the roast in another pot. He put the scraps back in the oven and took the roast to our next door neighbor and asked if she could keep it warm for him. When my mom got back she asked, "How is the roast?" He said, "Oh shoot, I forgot to look." She ran into the kitchen, opened the stove, and stared at small pieces of burnt meat. She started crying and said,

"What happened, why couldn't you watch this, it's ruined." My dad started laughing and told her what he did. She didn't think it was funny.

WE WENT OUT to the cotton field and after a few hours I needed to use the restroom so I headed to the house. While in the house, I saw a new bag of chocolate chip cookies on the kitchen counter and thought I would just eat a couple before going back. We picked cotton until lunch time and we all came in to eat. My grandmother saw the open bag of cookies and said, "Who got into these?"

I said, "I did, I was hungry."

She turned red and said, "Who told you you could have a cookie, those are for your grandfather's lunches. You stole cookies."

What I didn't know, was that besides farming, my grandfather worked part time at the post office. The little bit of cotton and peanuts they grew wasn't enough to support them.

My dad said, "What's wrong with you?"

"I didn't know," I said. He swatted me in the back of the head, almost knocking me out of my chair.

My life on the farm was not going well. Not only was I a lazy shit, a dumb ass, a scaredy cat, but now I was a thief.

SUNDAY CAME AND I was excited because we didn't have to pick cotton, it was a day of rest. My dad's brother, Max, was coming over with his family and there was going to be a lot of food. The table was full of chicken, ham, potato salad, corn on the cob, green beans, sticky rice, biscuits, lots if icetea, and watermelon.

The plan was to make homemade ice cream, which I soon learned was not an easy task. My uncle had brought an ice cream maker with a hand crank. My aunt had prepared the ingredients so all we had to do was add ice and rock salt and crank. We got to take turns turning the crank, my turn being pretty short since I tired out fast. It was the best ice cream I have ever had. While we were eating, my dad asked Max.

"So how is Ruby?"

"He's doing okay, stays up at his place mostly, don't see him much."

I whispered to Joe, "Who is Ruby?"

He said, "My dad."

Ruby, was my dad's other brother, the black sheep of the family. He lived like a hermit on a piece of land nearby. My dad also had two sisters. He was the oldest, then Ruby, then the two sisters whom I had never met, then Max. How my cousin came to live with my grandparents I never knew. Joe had an older sister, Barbara, that sometimes lived at my grandparents but since we were staying there had moved in with her mom for a while. This was all too complicated for me to figure out, so I after we ate, I said to Joe, "Let's go down to the creek."

My cousin had a pellet pistol that looked like a German luger, and he brought that with him. We walked down to the creek and he told me to watch out for water moccasins. We took off our shoes and socks and were splashing around when I looked down and saw a snake lying very still in the creek. I showed it to Joe, and he said, "That's a water moccasin. You want to shoot it?"

I said, "Yea." He handed me the pistol. I straddled the creek and looking straight down aimed and pulled the trigger. Water and mud sprayed all over me and as the water cleared the snake just swam off. My cousin was laughing so hard he had tears in his eyes.

"You did that on purpose," I yelled.

"You were stupid enough to try and shoot it."

I shot my cousin in the foot. He screamed and I grabbed my socks and shoes and started running back to the house. I could hear him behind me and ran even faster. One thing I have always been able to do, is out run anyone chasing me, maybe this is where I learned how.

I came flying into the yard, Joe right on my ass. Panting, I said, "We saw a snake!"

My mom said, "Are you okay?"

"I tried to shoot it, but I missed."

Joe said, " Yea, he hit my foot instead."

I looked over at him and he just shrugged, he had half a smile on his face, saying, *I will get you back*.

His foot was okay just red and a little bloody where the pellet hit him, My grandmother said, "Just go wash up, good thing he didn't shoot you in the eye."

LABOR DAY WEEKEND was coming and I learned that I would be going to school with Joe in a small place called Woodleaf. This was also where my grandfather worked at the post office. Besides the post office, a store, and the school, there wasn't much else. I was excited to find out that school would let out at one pm every day, at least for the month of September. But then I found out why. Most of the kids came from farms and had to help finish picking the cotton crop so the school accommodated by letting us out early.

There was a bus that picked us up off the highway, which meant we had to walk the mile from the farmhouse. And, naturally, walk the mile back each afternoon. The morning walk was fine but the later walk was hot, and the red dust was easy to kick up, so by the time we got home I was covered in it.

As I said, being a military brat, we move every few years. Usually, adjusting to a new place was not hard because we went to school on military bases and all the other kids were in the same boat. Here it was different. Most of the kids at this rural school had never been much farther than Salisbury, a town about seven miles away. They had all grown up together, making me a total oddity to them. Not only had I lived in several other states, but here I was waiting to go to Africa. The teacher took this as an opportunity to teach about Morocco and had me stand up in front of the class and talk about the places I had lived. They all thought I was a rich kid who got to travel and see the world, while all the time I was jealous that they got to live in one place.

When school let out, we hopped on the bus, and then walked back to the farmhouse. We went straight out to the field and when my grandpa saw us he said, "Joe, you and Bill go grab the tractor and bring the flatbed over here."

One of the great things about farming, is that my cousin was allowed to drive a tractor at the age of nine. We ran over to the barn and hooked the flatbed to the tractor and he jumped in the seat. He said, "You sit up here on the back fender and I'll drive." I positioned myself on the lip of the fender and held on as we started toward the field. He got the tractor moving at a pretty good pace. When we were almost to the cotton field he swerved hard and gunned it. I went flying off the side and landed on my back in the dirt. I couldn't breathe, having the wind knocked out of me. He stopped the tractor and said, "C'mon sissy, you're okay. That was for shooting me in the foot."

I managed to get up, and said, " Okay, so now we're even?" He said, "Yea", and I climbed back on.

BY THE END of September the cotton was in and my mom started complaining about having to stay with my grandparents. She was a city girl and was not adapting to the country. I think she was just bored. There wasn't much for her to do except keep an eye on my three-year-old sister. My dad agreed to rent an apartment in Salisbury until we left for North Africa.

We found a place that could hold all of us and it just so happened it was right up the street from a foot-long hot dog place. A twelve-inch hot dog, smothered with chili, onions, ketchup, mustard, relish, on a fresh bun. I was in heaven. It was here that my mom found one of her recipes that I was to enjoy for a long time. One option at the hot dog place, was to run chile down one side of the hot dog and coleslaw down the other. The combination is delicious and my mother made it at home for us over the years.

One night when we were eating at our apartment, my older sister and I got in an argument over a bottle of ketchup. We had both reached for it at the same time and neither of us was letting go. My dad said, "Knock it off", and hit me in the chest with his fist. I couldn't breathe and fell face first onto my plate. My mom jumped up and cried, "You killed him!" I came to gulping air and spitting out pieces of the hamburger I had been trying to eat. My dad said, "He's fine, I just knocked the wind out of him."

My mom said, "Don't you ever touch him again!" I had never heard her stand up to my dad like that, and was sorry it had to be on my account.

That incident pretty much sealed the deal in my relationship with my father. He never wanted to have much to do with me after that. So in a few short months I had established myself as a lazy shit, a dumb ass, a scaredy cat, a thief, and finally, a momma's boy.

Just before Thanksgiving, the orders came through for us to head to Casablanca. We packed up the Chevy and drove to New York where the government would take it and have it shipped for us. We boarded a twin engine Gooney bird which is a Douglas DC-3/C47 airplane and were off, with a fuel stop in the Azores, and then to Morocco for the next chapter of my life

DARK

Father and Son

Expectation, falling short.
   Conversation, never expressed.

   Measurement, always less.
Failure, trying my best.

Love, seldom shown.
Achievement, missing the mark.

Feelings, never known.
Emotion, cold and dark.

Confidence, small and shaken.
Admiration, lost and broken.

Time, stealing the hope of reclamation.

Death closing the door to reconciliation.

A Soul Bound

Thoughts race unspoken,
    Emotions burn unexpressed.
    Outward, signs of togetherness.
    Inward, cracked and broken.

    Waves of depression offset
    by peaks of exhilaration.
    Moments of jubilation
    washed away, being upset.

    Nerve endings longing,
    Imagination straining,
    Fantasy exploding,
    Desire unending.

    A bottle with sides opaque.
    Outside, a calm form.
    Inside, like a storm.
    A heart wanting to break.

    A gap unable to cross,

A void lost in thought,
A need never caught,
A life ending in loss.

To The Past

Cold and sober lies the stone.
    In loving memory it begins,
    With simple dates of birth
    and death, it ends.
    Now, once again, she lies alone.
    My mind races to remember.
    Thoughts fail to paint past pictures,
    Memories fail to recall one grand adventure.
    Only the stone reminds,
    Her birth was December.

Sadness plays at my soul.
She lived a life too short to see
Her only son grow to maturity.
The circle of her life failed to be whole.
Standing over the grave, the stone,
Feelings within fail to appear,
Except, only that she is no longer here.
Nothing left but to, again, leave her alone.

From Light Into Dark

Backing away from the brightness
    Moving gradually into gray.
    Time slipping unstoppable,
    Distance increasing from the light.

    Awareness, awakening, comes too late.
    Surroundings unfamiliar, strange.
    Life moving oddly forward,
    White to gray to black.

    Depression, hardness, loneliness,
    Feelings failing to enlighten,
    Darkness compressing, suffocation.
    Light retreats, dark prevails.

False Image

Like a mirage floating on
   the desert sand,
   A reflection flashing quickly
   through the corner of your eye.

   A perception dissolving in the
   light of truth.
   The false image lingers, holding on,
   controlling.

Not real, not true, only living
out of hope, and false belief.
Empty, cold, yet clutching,
holding back, strangling.

Pray for strength to break this false vision
Cry out for light to flood in an image of reality
Hope that truth can break the chains of this life.
May the false image be unveiled.

Guilt

The sky is brightly blue,
    Yet the focus is on one lone cloud.
    Sun overhead burning red,
    Thoughts remind of the night's shroud.

    Energy is high as possibilities rise.
    Doubt begins to drain, slowing the flow.
    Present and past provide hope,
    Future thoughts of I don't know.

    Life intended to live and enjoy.
    Moods rise and fall, missing the ecstasy.
    Love lifts the soul.
    The face frowning, eyes fail to see.

    One word causes all to tilt.
    One phrase repeating, guilt, guilt, guilt…

Abused

Broken, like the fragile
   wing of a bird.
   Wounded, like a deer
   in the sight of the hunter.

   Afraid, like the lost cub
   too far from the den.
   Hurt, like the squirrel clipped
   by the moving vehicle.

Alone, like the kitten
left in the rain.

As she looks back she can only feel
Broken, wounded, afraid, hurt, alone.

Her only hope, to reach within
and slowly turn
To what lies ahead.

Dilemma

If he had a highly infectious disease
   would he not be in quarantine?
   If he was labeled a menace to society
   would he not be incarcerated?

   Then, why when he could take his
   life and the lives of my offspring
   No one reacts, no one does a thing?

   When the headlines appear describing
   the loss of three lives,
   They will gather around and say
   "We saw the potential,
   We knew this would happen."

   My fear goes unnoticed,
   My cries go unheard,
   My prayer seems unanswered,
   My future remains blurred.

What can I do? What can I say?
Each moment suspended,
All hope gone away.

For Christ's Sake

Over Jerusalem you wept
    Saddened to see the city of David deny.

    Recovering you told them to go out
    from here, to Samaria, to all of Judea,
    to the uttermost parts of the earth.

    Now over the world you weep,
    Saddened to see, they heard, yet still they deny.

From Shepherd To Snake

They gathered together,
   Singing, praising, praying,
   Waiting for a word from God.

   A word that would bring
   Hope, comfort, challenge.
   Making their path easier to trod.

   The shepherd led them,
   Encouraging, caring, sharing
   Answers in a world confused.

   Always there, for each of them,
   Grieving, hurting, crying
   As life continued to abuse.

   The shepherd fed them,
   Teaching, praying, preaching
   The words they needed to hear.

They knew on him they could count,
Listening, advising, loving.
He was always, always near.

The shepherd taught them grace,
The law no longer in command.
With him they reached out to others,
Helping with a helping hand.

Like sheep, protected, cared for,
No longer gone astray.
They could face anything, except
Their shepherd going away.

They had been blind, at least
Chose not to see
His hurt, his pain, his tears,
His life of misery.

One day he stood before them
Saying he could no longer lead.
He hoped he had made a difference,

Putting into their lives, at least a seed.

They promised to still love him.
They were sad to see him go.
They said they would pray for him
And, that they would miss him so.

With that the shepherd left them.
Barely had he gone out the door,
When their faces shifted quickly,
The shepherd was no more.

Their promises were empty, no one
Called or wrote or cared.
The shepherd had only moved on,
They acted like he had disappeared.
 To them he was no longer a shepherd.
What difference now could he make?
To them he was non existent,
To them he had become a snake.

As The Light Dims

Forbidden fruit calling out
    Promising to awaken, to enlighten.

    Destiny demanding response, action.
    Was it anyone's fault?
    Was it not meant to be?

    The struggle begins,
    Blood is sacrificed,
    Balance restored.

    Now, once again knowledge is forbidden,
    Ignorance has a new voice.

    Cries for awakening abound.
    How can this be?
    Can you not hear the contradiction?

    How can awakening burst forth
    From slumber?

When the elixir of narrowness
Is all we have to drink.

When all we can eat is the food
Of hatred, of conformity.

Gifts of the spirit are hidden, unopened,
Tucked neatly away.

Replaced by rules, regulations,
By mind control.

Love has been lost, the gates
Of the garden are closed,
Once again

Gray

The Roller Coaster

Life, twisting, turning,
              Spiraling ever downward.

  Love, exciting, thrilling,
              Lifting ever upward.

Duty holding close,
              Grasping life's track.

Desire pulling out,
              Tugging to pull back.

Obligation pressing,
              Pushing one to sit down.

Freedom exploding,
              Calling one to be unbound.

Emotions of guilt

Speeding, acting like a bar.

Eros demanding
        Expression from afar.

Joy, peace, comfort
        Lifting higher and higher.

Sadness, worry, questions
        Pushing lower and lower.

Time causing the ride
        To end too soon.

Time providing moments
        Under the sun and moon.

Will this last forever
        Or eventually subside?
Excuse me sir —
        Give us one more ticket to ride.

Reality

Glances exchanged
    Moments stolen.

    Words hidden,
    Conversation broken.

    Love forbidden,
    Love unspoken.

    Life together,
    Life unbroken.

Duality

Confusion, chaos, anxiety,
   Peace, calm, serenity.

   Stress, hassle, harassment,
Joy, love, contentment.

   Harsh words, intimidation.
Soft voices, communication.

   Tension, defenses raised.
Freedom, attributes praised.

   Bitterness, heartlessness,
Passion caresses.

   Lies, deceit, deception.
Truth, honesty, reception.

   Rejection, pain, agony.
Acceptance, grace, ecstasy.

Choices forbidden, actions dictated.
Choices abounding, actions appreciated.

A life of sadness, sorrow.
A life of looking forward to tomorrow.

The duality of life laid before.
Choose, now and forevermore.

Stepfather

Feeling love within one's heart,
    Stifling touch, staying apart.
    Concern and care cautiously expressed.
    Boundaries placed, lines often pressed.

    Confusion accepted, even understood.
    But my heart is flesh, not wood.
    Daddy, a name not to hear.
    Only hope, is to just be there.

Sadness, when the other man fails.
Trying not to counter with better tales.
Knowing no way to ever replace,
Hoping only for my own small place.

A place somewhere within their hearts,
Playing in their lives, at least a part.

Perplexed

Reality presents the truth,
    Imagination creates a false scenario.
    Life unfolds moment after moment,
    Anxiety tries to mold it just so.

    Possibilities abound in hope.
    Fear emerges, ceasing the flow.
    Night arrives so rest can begin,
    Mind continues to stir, it won't let go.

    Variety adding flavor to life,
    Too many unknowns to know.
    Reality, life, possibilities, night,
    Variety, all should create a glow.

    Maybe love will be the answer,
    Maybe love will free her soul.

The Play of Life - Act One

It could be a play by Tennessee Williams,
    Roles played out with intense passion.
    Or songs by Rogers and Hammerstein,
    Sung to lift the spirits from depression.
    It could be, but it is not.

    It would be if it were not
    For the play already played.
    Perhaps the play was first by Shakespeare,
    Perhaps the song was done by Bach.
    It could be, but it is not.

    The play came before, perhaps
    A tragedy played out in Rome.
    The songs were sung with Nero
    Fiddling, as fires burned.
    It could be, but it is not.

    The play has been since time began,
    A story, repetitious, from the first curtain.
    Only the players have changed.

The songs were sung when forces first heard,
The tune the same,
The words only slightly altered.

The play, the song, one act, one tune,
Changing only by who gets to act,
By who gets to sing.
The critics, of course, never quite catching on!

Choice

The roads we take,
    The turns we make,
    Make life a pain or
    Make life a break.

    The roads not traveled
    Blur our vision, play
    On our eyes a trick.

    We think they would
    Be paved with gold.
    They're actually only made
    Of yellow brick.

    The roads we take
    The turns we make
    Are all meant to be enjoyed.
    To not, is our mistake.

Why?

Why do you love me? My lover asks.

  Had she my eyes
               She could see why,

  Had she my soul,
               She would know why.

  Why, would not be a question
               If she were me.

  Her beauty stops my heart,
               Takes my breath.

  Her smile charms, disarms,
               Brightens my day.

  Her wit brings a smile,
               Causes me to pause,

Her grace deceives,
> Hiding passion within.

Her gaze tells me
> She loves me,

Her ears listen when
> I share my thoughts.

Her touch floods my
> Soul, energizing,

Her heart cares for
> My well-being.

Her mind is quick
> Matching thought for thought.

Her movement draws
> Me even closer,

Her ankles call out,

        Luring me in,

Her mouth
        Is an endless kiss.

Why do I love her?
        How could I not!

To My Sister-In-Law

She had given herself over to the night,
    Letting darkness overpower her own light.
    Idleness, amazingly had control over
    Desire, creativity, self worth.

    Stagnate, she stood, sad, alone,
    Asking how did this come about?
    Blame seeking a place to land, to take hold.
    Only the truth splashed like a cold slap,
    It was her decision, or the lack thereof.

    Slowly strength returned, confidence restored.
    Saying "Adios," "Good-bye," "Sayonara."
    Claim restored upon her own soul.
    Life begins, continues anew, now whole,
    The day dawns with hope.

Alone

Alone, I sit in her room,
    Running my fingers on the cover of her bed.
    Imagining, remembering things she has said.
    Alone, I sit in her room.

Alone, I sit in her room
Staring at the simple things of her life,
Wanting to be a part of her life.
Alone, I sit in her room.

Alone, I sit in her room
The feel, the scent, bring her to mind,
Hoping as I close my eyes, her to find.
Alone, I sit in her room.

Alone, I sit in her room,
Alone, it is cold, empty, sad.
When she returns my heart will be glad.
Alone, I sit in her room.

Memo

To: Christianity

>Halloween called a Fall Festival
>Is but still, just Halloween.
>Rock and Roll tunes sung to Jesus
>Are but still, just Rock and Roll.
>Build your fortress,
>Condemn the world,
>The walls will not save you.
>The world laughs in your face.
>Hide in the church basement,
>For sex is at the door,
>Bolt the double doors,
>They want to dance on your floor.
>Pray for salvation,
>In a world gone mad,
>Evil is everywhere,
>All good is now bad.
>Banish those who watch TV,
>Shun any who might disagree.
>Be pure, moral, upright, clean.

Be righteous, perfect,
Say nothing mean.

Or
Maybe you should
Take a second look
At your Bible, your rule book.
Maybe, just maybe,
It might be better,
If you saw the Bible
As a love letter.

From: God.

The Right

He loved
They hate
He was calm
They are angry
He forgave
They condemn
They say they believe in Him.

He spoke gently
They shout
He healed
They wound
He united
They divide
They say they believe in Him.

He served
They control
He listened
They ignore
He was humble
They are proud

They say they believe in Him.

They say they believe in Him
They say they work in His name
They say they follow Him
I wonder what He will say to them.

The Optimist In A Democracy

"Two steps forward, one step back."
   The good life, seemingly ever so close.
   But, once again, you find yourself under attack!

The wheel of life spins once again.
You've put your hopes on number eleven.
The wheel slows to a stop…… on ten.

One by one you had removed your debts.
One more to go, life about to be free and clear.
The taxman steps up and says,
 "You want to bet?"

Back to square one, do not pass go.
The cycle of life begins anew.
Any chance for you to get ahead, just ain't so.

A New Beginning

Worry replaced by peace.
   Cold removed by love.
   Anxiety dissipates into calm.

   Fear growing into joy.
   Dark moving into light.
   Doubt overcome by trust.

   Slowly, gradually, eventually,
   Life begins to turn.
   New life, new love.

   A new beginning.

LIGHT!

Into The Light

A flower growing
   In the shadow of the rock.

   Buds not quite fully opening,
   The sun never reaching the petals.

   In a world defined by darkness
   Only degrees of shade, never light.

   A flower, mature at first glance,
   A flower, never able to fully blossom.

   Suddenly, the earth quakes,
   The ground begins to move.

   The rock rolls away,
   The flower stands fully exposed.

   The brightness of the sun

Floods across where only darkness stood.

The flower begins to grow,
The blossoms open unafraid.

The stem straightens, the petals
Reach up to the sun.

The flower realizes life as
It was meant to be,

No longer lingering in the
Shadow of the rock.

In Search of Love

A thirst, water could only
   Soothe, never quench.

   A burning, calmed but
   Quickly rekindled.

   A desire, seemingly met,
   Yet never fulfilled.

   Then came a special water,
   A unique slave,
   A completion of desire.

No longer thirsty,
No longer aflame,
No longer longing.

At peace, at rest, content,
Life now fulfilled.

Love Finally Found

Images of the past swirl,
>Veiling enjoyment of the present.

Words spoken anew, yet
>Thinking old meanings meant.

Two hearts commonly searching
>For one love .

Two minds grasping for moments
>Granted from above.

Common ground, standing each
>With love never found.

Hesitant now to accept
>Hearts afraid to go unbound.

Passion rises, hearts begin to race.

The moment, suddenly broken,
> They are in the wrong place.

Both hopeful, eyes looking
> Above for a sign.

Prayers expressed to bind
> Both heart and mind.

Two lives, now complete,
> Wanting only love to share.

God protect them, guide,
> Let them know…love is there.

At Half Moon Bay

The fog horn bellows,
    Time stretches, or is it that
    One just slows to feel the seconds.
    Gulls squawk as the sound of the waves repeats.
    The fog horn bellows.

    The fishermen stand among the rocks,
    Lines baited with hope, set with patience,
    As the surfers wait.
    The fog horn bellows.

    A wave appears carrying reward
    As now the fishermen reel in,
    The surfer atop his board floats home.
    The fog horn bellows.

    Lovers walk alone, along the crowded beach,
    Sandpipers play tag with endless tides.
    The sun falls off the edge of the earth.
    The fog horn bellows.

Night brings calm as the fishermen retreat
The surfers disappear,
Flying off with the sandpipers.
The lovers draw closer as the gulls settle down.
The fog horn bellows.

Red

Red as a blazing sunset
    Across the hot desert sand.
    Red as the ever increasing
    Octagon that impedes our progress.
    Red as the blush of the young
    As thoughts of sharing enter their minds.
    Red as the fabric that
    Enrages the beast.
    Red as the flora named
    By scribes of yore.
    Red as the life giving fluid
    That flows within.
    Red as the glow shining
    From the heart of secret treasure.
    Red as the gentle lace,
    Gathered to enhance.
    Red, red, red, red,
    Red, red, red, red.

The Bay

Once a quiet place,
    Spanish being the first to reside.

Fishermen daily casting their nets.
Work, scheduled along with the tide.

Peaceful, serene, calm,
An occasional visitor out for a Sunday ride.

Along came a man, many knew,
Capturing the bay, making it known.

Suddenly, a place discovered,
Flocks streaming to where the birds had flown.

Change taking place as
The seeds of greed and growth were sown.

Still, this is a place of memories,
Of days past and thoughts being sent.

Change, however, cannot change what
God has placed, though man tries to rent.

Yet for all its beauty, all its charm,
Until now, time there was sadly spent.

Now the bay is brighter,
Now the air is clear.

Now the ocean roars louder,
Now the sunsets seem so near.

Now the birds fly higher,
Now the waves hold no fear.

Whole days of exploring, walking,
Sharing the life of the bay,

Have been abundant.
One thing is added this day.

For all the words ever expressed,

There was one this poet could not say.

Love has been added,
Love has been found.

To the bay love has been given,
Lovers now walk, feet on the ground.

The bay has become a symbol
A place where love now abounds.

What the bay thought was lost
Was discovered to be in reach.

The bay helped lovers discover
That love could come to each.

Lovers now know love will remain,
As long as lovers never leave
The other's piano on the beach.

Renewal

Eyes able, once
                Again, to see
   Ears listening to
                Words so clear.

A mind that now
                Thinks above the fog.
Air, refreshing
                Filling the lungs.

A heart beating
                Strong, alive.
A soul no longer
                Content with the past.

A life ready to
                Live, experience.

The chain has been broken.

Face To Face

Sensation, erupting deep within the soul.
   Emotion, racing, confusing
   The logic of the mind.

   Forces, pulling, wanting to be in motion.
   Blood, raging, pounding,
   Eyes about to go blind.

   The prophet cries,
   "Fire in my bones!"
   The man burns with un-quenching desire.

   The spirit strains to remain calm,
   The flesh igniting passion,
   Like fire.

   Time suspends, reality fades,
   Vision unfocused, thought dissolves,
   Passion explodes, love erupts.

Desire releases, mystery solved.
She is before him, her beauty astounds.
He is before her, his love abounds.

The Shelf

They stand side by side
                Arranged by lines.

King, Melville, Koontz,
                Tolkien, Einstein.

Men in mutiny, on an isle
                Of bounty,

Hobbits, thinkers, and gremlins,
                Mixing with a dictionary.

Words creating many thoughts,
                Many stories.
Words expressing one expression.

All these variations uniting,
                Describing one man's passion.

Technology

Is it you and I or you and me?
   Is it layed, laid, or lay?
   Or is it stayed, staid, or stay?

   Not to worry,
   Press enter and it will be clear,
   The grammar program will fix the error.

   Is it pease or piece?
   Or is it poose or pose?
   Is it knew or nu?
   Or is it shows or shose

   Not to worry,
   Press enter and it will be clear,
   Spell check will fix the error.

   OOPS, the power went out!
   Howe may I finnesh this pome?

My Heart

Words have been written,
   Words have been spoken.

   No two lovers, ever more smitten,
   No two hearts ever more broken.

   Ours is a love like the world
   Has never seen.
   A love with ripples that
   Some would consider mean.

   Yet, know that only God
   With His love so true

   Can ever begin to match
   The love I have for you.

To Cathryn

Light crests over the hillside,
   Darkness slowly dissipates.

   Love moves in like the tide,
   Washing over the sands of bitterness.

   Joy, shining like a bright evening star,
   Changes the face of a night of sadness.

   Passion ignites like lightening on a dry forest,
   Obliterating thoughts of loneliness.

   All of this is swirling, mixing,
   Changing to make me whole.

   Filling, the once empty box
   I called my soul.

Love and Struggle

Life is an intertwining
    Of love and struggle.
    Out of love we are created,
    Out of struggle we are born.

    Love nurtures as we grow,
    Struggle molds as we mature.
    Love causes us to seek another,
    Struggle binds us to each other.

    When struggle strains to overcome
    Love tips the scales,
    Balance is maintained.

    When love tries to stand alone
    Only fantasy remains,
    Struggle is inevitable.

    It is only when true love is found
    That struggles become surmountable.

True love intertwined with struggle,
Makes a life worth the living,
Makes a life truly enjoyable.

Step One of A Marriage

"Like two spoons lying in a drawer."
    Like pieces of a puzzle designed to interlock.
    Soulmates having found one another,
    Love creating a foundation out of rock.

    Life is a series of givens, of unknowns.
    Life is a balance of pleasure, of pain.
    Unknowns can now be faced, pain can be withstood,
    Love finally a pleasure, love finally a given.

    Time short-changed a life together
    Yet time remains to share each other.
    Love now found eases loves lost.
    Commitment now held, forgetting the cost.

    The past stands, forever unchanged,
    A future together, in hope it remains.
    Sound, touch, smell, taste,
    Combining emotions, nothing gone to waste.

Moments to hold, arms to embrace.
Years not guaranteed, yet life now able to face.
Love is expressed hour by hour,
Love now realized, now we feel its power.

About The Author

I was born
   In the red hills
   Of Carolina in the South
   But called North.
   The year coincided
   With the first UFO sighting,
   Coincidence? Or maybe my
   Stork was traveling at warp speed.

Highpoint was the city
And in days of depression
Seems to be the only one in life.
But, then maybe not, for
My life is one of contrast
And opposites that attract.

Fear of God never as strong
As the fear caused by "The Blood of Dracula",
Causing a young man to spread
Garlic on the windowsill.
Born into a family where
Discipline, saluting, and
Weapons of destruction were
The bread and butter that
Put the ketchup on the table.
A bottle over which my older

Sister and I fought, ending
With me face down in my plate,
A result of a father who had
A good right hook, which because
He loved baseball made mine
Come from the left.

A father who desperately
Hoped for a son who one
Day would take the mound and
Be the white Sachel Paige,
Only to discover a boy with
An arm meant more to hold
A pen than a ball and who
Mounted, not a mound but a pulpit.
Memory recalling my father's mitt
Flying toward my head,
But the speed of sound was faster
As his words hit first,
"You're useless."

A dad whose passion seemed to be
To fish and to hunt until his son
Came of age and could accompany,
Could participate.
In spite of this rejection, at ten
With a .22 and tin cans was a crack shot.
A Scout who would be quartermaster and
When the cry went out, "Where's the beef?"
Could respond, "On my back."

Called a military brat, not
Just a brat like most,
Never able to send roots
Deep enough to take hold
Tumbling like a tumbleweed,
Stopping for short spurts.
Then as the wind of change
Grew strong, rolling on to
The next enclosed enclosure,
Separated by chain link and barbed wire
From tradition and community,
And the girl next door, who you
Could watch develop and long for.

Brain cells, affected early on as
We as a gang, rode on bikes
Behind a government pick-up
In a cloud of DDT sprayed to
Protect our neighborhood.
The trade off being toys of youth
That were weapons of mass destruction
That a young boy could crawl through
And play around while the old man,
"Sarge", they called him, ordered,
Directed, and saluted.

The trade-off being surrounded by locusts

At ten in a strange land of
Mosques, veils, and strange writing
That resembled snakes curling this way
And that way. Cities like Rabat
And Marrakech, when other boys
Never left the farm. An education
By the street, teaching me how foolish
To stage a sling shot fight with Arab boys,
Slinging since David felled Goliath.

At a time when Howdy Doody, Buffalo Bob,
And Elvis slither across the vast wasteland.
An older sister too young to drive
Giving birth and leaving the nest.
Tragedy falling as a young eighth grader
Is taken from class, "Your grandfather is dead".
Years would pass before
The boy, turned man, would
Understand Grandpa was the only male who
Related to him, as a male.
Now the oldest, with still a younger
One behind, given charge of cleaning
Up the mess to white glove perfection.

Lust fulfilled not by the girl
Who lived next door,
But by looking at older women, friends of the
Family, well endowed, older, but
Not so old to allow young man's fancy
Grow to fantasy. Finally fantasy played out

In reality as my first love, Jeannie Craig at 12,
Listened to by my pubescent voice sing out with
"Won't you wear my ring around your neck?
And show the world you're mine by heck."

My next major love, Marsha Street, adorned
In a waist length pigtail, her weapon.
Sticks and stones may break my bones
But that pigtail could knock me out.
Suddenly, she chose to cut it,
Suddenly, I was cut off.

The sounds of dad screaming failure,
Disappointment, as reality crushed his
Field of dreams and conversation never
Expressed until the day I, too, adorned
Stripes and marched to a different drummer.
Guarding Philadelphia while fellow
Countryman fell in a different jungle.
Strange how guilt creeps
In by not dying alongside.

Change and renovation a way of life
That brought understanding and compassion
For all things different, and ready
For things spontaneous. Not ever
Accepting "just because". Asking "why?" and
Why not? Not afraid of authority but,

Too quick to move on, to close out,
To shut down, too eager to change
For the sake of change. Settling in
But not settling down.

Looking for love in all the wrong places,
But then they say the third time is the charm.
Wife number one hit an early grave
As alcohol consumed her soul.
Wife number two caught by the same desire.

For everyone there is a perfect match,
So fate finally took control
And a soulmate found.
The left hand created to pitch now writes
And a life of change has now
Become a good routine.